Table of Contents

Such was the darkness of that day, the tortures and lamentations of the Afflicted and the power of former precedents, that we walked in the clouds and could not see our way.

— Rev.John Hale of Beverly

A Climate of Fear

For eight months in 1692 Essex County went on a witch hunt. From March to September, several hundred persons were cried out against. One hundred seventeen women and thirty-nine men were accused and imprisoned. Within a four month period fourteen women and five men were hanged and one old man was pressed to death.

It was not the only outbreak of witch hysteria in New England. Sixteen had previously been put to death for this crime and hundreds more accused over the past forty-five years. Salem is the most famous because it came late in the history of witch hunts; took place within a relatively short span of time; and many people who had been there wrote about what they had witnessed.

Nearly everyone in the 17th Century believed in witchcraft and the power of the supernatural, the "Invisible World of Spirits." In 1604, English Parliament under King James I passed an act making the practice of witchcraft punishable on the first offense. The Puritans brought this Biblical law "Thou shalt not suffer a witch to live" (Exodus 22:18) to Massachusetts Bay Colony, along with their Old World folk traditions.

A witch was someone pledged to serve Satan by performing his evil deeds in this world. They made a contract by signing the Devil's Book in exchange for special powers like flying and performing feats of super strength. Their mischief caused the sudden death of a cow, a child's illness, and failure to prosper. People may have wondered why some of their neighbors were accused and others were not, but they never doubted the existence of witches.

"Wicked Sorceries Have Been Practiced in the Land"

It started in Salem Village, now the town of Danvers. The minister's frail nine-year-old daughter, Betty, and her cousin, eleven-year-old Abigail Williams, were confined inside the house during this particularly cold winter assigned to household chores and Scripture reading. Tituba, a slave brought from Barbados, where the Rev. Samuel Parris had failed in business, enlivened the girls' days with tales and folklore from her West Indian island. Their friends, twelve-year-old Anne Putnam and Mercy Lewis, Mary Warren, Mary Wolcott, and other teenage servant girls, several of whom had been orphaned by Indian attacks, also knew fortune-telling games from centuries of European tradition. And they knew that such "wicked, little sorceries" were against the rules of their strict Puritan society.

> In their vain curiosity to know their future condition, they tampered with the devil's tools.
>
> — The Rev. John Hale, "A Modest Enquiry into the Nature of Witchcraft and How Persons Guilty of that Crime May be Convicted. And the Means Used for their Discovery Discussed ... According to Scriptures & Experiences" (Boston, 1702).

One of their favorite magic tricks was to drop the white of an egg in a glass of water. The shape it took was supposed to tell the vocation of a girl's future husband. When Betty Parris recognized "a specter in the likeness of a coffin," she became hysterical with fear and guilt. Betty and her cousin, Abigail, soon began to behave strangely. They writhed on the floor, moaned, shrieked and barked like dogs. Abigail even pulled burning sticks from the fireplace, threw them about the room and attempted to fly up the chimney. The village doctor, William Griggs, examined the girls and made a terrifying diagnosis: "The Evil Hand is upon them." Other village girls also experienced convulsions. They spoke gibberish, flung their arms and legs about, screamed and swore, and refused to say their prayers.

At first the girls refused to tell who had afflicted them, but the adults kept coaxing them to identify the witches living among them. Finally, they offered the names of three women who fit the witch stereotype: women from the bottom rung of the social ladder who had long been unpopular in Salem Village. Sarah Good, the foul-mouthed, homeless, beggar woman; old Sarah Osborne, who'd had three husbands and was accused of witchcraft years before; and Parris' slave, Tituba. They were arrested the first week of March and questioned by magistrates John Hathorne and Jonathan Corwin at the Meetinghouse. As the frightened women attempted to answer the judges' questions, the girls went into fits.

> The children were bitten and pinched by invisible agents; their arms, necks, and backs turned this way and that way, and returned back again, so as it was impossible for them to do of themselves and by the power of any epileptic fits, or natural disease to effect.
> — The Rev. John Hale, "A Modest Enquiry Into the Nature of Witchcraft..."

After being beaten by Parris, Tituba confessed. "The devil came to me and bid me serve him," she told the magistrates. Futhermore, there were other witches around town tormenting the girls, as well as a "tall man from Boston." Tituba said that Sarah Good had a yellow bird, a wolf, and a cat for Familiars, while Osborne had one with wings and a woman's head and another, "all over hairy." She described riding through the air on a stick to attend witch meetings.

When the Afflicted Girls began to name respected church members, panic set in. The church no longer provided protection against witchcraft. "Christ knows how many Devils there are among us!" Sermons like this preached by the Rev. Samuel Parris encouraged the witch hunt by teaching that Satan could not take over an innocent person. Parris' Salem Village congregation was already divided. Many were against his ministry and had long refused to pay their share of firewood and farm provisions towards his salary.

Salem Village, an agricultural parish with a population of 550, had separated from Salem Town in 1672. The villagers resented the wealthy seaport's political and economic control over their local affairs. There had also been long-standing hostilities among neighbors as well as old family rivalries. Now such hassles over lands and grudges against old enemies could be used as evidence in court.

Massachusetts Bay Colony had been founded upon the Puritan's belief that they made a covenant with God to set up "Cities in the Wilderness." Now, fifty years after the Great Migration to create this utopian society based upon the Bible, everything seemed to be going wrong. Theirs was now a country without rule.

The clergy, long their educated guides on the Path to Salvation, were losing influence. The colony was in legal limbo, without any workable judicial system. The Royal Charter, granted by King Charles I, had given the Mass Bay Colonists the authority to govern themselves. It had been revoked by the Crown in 1684. The Rev. Increase Mather had been sent to England to negotiate a new Colonial Charter.

Attacks by Native Americans, allied with the French, had become increasingly frightening and frequent. Indeed, from 1688-1761, Colonists and Native Americans were pawns in the struggle between England and France for the rule of the North American Continent. This fear and violence was also based on cultural differences. The Puritans thought Native Americans, with their painted faces and pagan worship, were the Devil's agents.

If after anger between neighbors mischief followed, this oft bred suspicion of witchcraft in the matter.

— The Rev. John Hale, "A Modest Enquiry Into the Nature of Witchcraft..."

The hunger to own land had brought the Puritans to the New World and now, as coastal settlements became more populated, boundary disputes increased. Many feared losing their land without any legal protection. They did not want to become tenants, bound to farm someone else's lands, as many had been in England.

Several smallpox epidemics devastated New England in the 1680s and 1690s and recent droughts had resulted in poor harvests. For Puritans who believed that God's Hand was in everything that happened, all these events were sure signs of His displeasure with them. As their political, economic, and religious institutions seemed to be crumbling, they looked for someone to blame for this instability of their society.

Sarah Osborne had already died in the Boston jail awaiting trial, when the Rev. Increase Mather arrived in Boston May 14, 1692 with the Crown's newly appointed Governor, Sir William Phips and the new Royal Charter. They were amazed to find the jails already jammed with prisoners accused of witchcraft.

Since no legal process for any crimes could take action until the new Charter took effect the following October, the new Governor set up on June 2, a special Court of Oyer et Terminer (To Hear and Determine) according to English law, to deal solely with witchcraft cases, naming William Stoughton Chief Justice. This intensified the accusations, since until new legislature could be put into place, this court represented the only recourse then available to Massachusetts Bay citizens with any legal complaints. Governor Phips promptly departed the Colony to lead a military expedition on the Eastern Frontier in Maine against the French and their Native American allies.

Bridget Bishop, who had been accused of witchcraft in 1678, was the first to go on trial before this Court of Oyer Et Terminer. She was convicted and swiftly hanged at Gallows Hill in Salem on June 10. At Court, Samuel Gray said he awakened one night to see Bridget Bishop's specter hovering over his child's cradle who "did then pine away and die." Judge Nathaniel Saltonstall resigned from Court because he disagreed with Bridget ("Goody") Bishop being condemned on the Afflicted Girls' hallucinations. He was also against their conviction of Rebecca Nurse, whose long life as a good Christian, he thought, had been disregarded. (Soon after his return home to Haverhill, he too would be accused by the Afflicted Girls.)

How to Identify a Witch

It was believed that Satan employed witches to inflict harm upon people after tempting them to make a covenant with him by promising them supernatural powers and material goods. Witches then did his bidding after renouncing Christian baptism, being rebaptized by Satan, and signing the Devil's Book with their blood. Witches supposedly gathered at night to hold devil-worshipping festivals at which they celebrated services that mocked Christ's sacred ceremony of Communion with bread and wine. A curse from a witch could bring injury upon a victim's body, livestock, or property. Two witnesses testifying that they had seen the accused or his or her familiar making a pact with Satan, or had been hurt by them, was enough court evidence for conviction of witchcraft. Kinfolk of accused witches were also frequently named as malefactors, since witchcraft supposedly ran in families.

Witches were aided by familiars, which were demons or imps, given to the witch by the Devil as assistants. These were usually small creatures, such as birds, snakes or cats.

After preliminary hearings, those arrested for witchcraft were made to suffer the humiliation of a strip and search by court-appointed persons, for Devil's Marks, also accepted as evidence by the court. This might be any wart, mole or birthmark upon the body from which familiars supposedly sucked nourishment. Pins might be stuck into such blemishes to discover a witch. Any painful reaction determined innocence.

An accuser points to a flock of birds she sees fluttering around the accused witch's head in this painting by Howard Pyle.

Witches might have poppets, dolls or waxen images that represented the Afflicted, that they might have twisted or stuck pins into to cause pain. Mary Bridges, Jr., one Afflicted Andover teenager, confessed, "I afflicted people by sticking pins into things and clothes, while thinking of hurting them. The dead taught me this way of afflicting."

Ann Foster of Andover confessed, "Goody Carrier came to me and would have me bewitch two children of Andrew Allen's. I had two puppets made, and stuck pins in them to bewitch the children. One of the children died, and the other became very sick. I tied a knot in a rag and threw it into the fire to hurt a Salem Village woman...."

A typical report on identifying witches by searching and testing for "witchmarks" follows:

> We whose names are underwritten having received an order from the sheriff to search the bodies of George Burroughs and George Jacobs, we find nothing upon the body of the above said Burroughs but what is natural, but upon the body of George Jacobs, we find 3 teats which according to the best of our Judgments we think is not natural for we run a pin through 2 of them and he was not sensible of it. One of them being within his mouth upon the Inside of his right cheek and 2nd upon his right shoulder blade and a 3rd upon his right hip.

> "View of Bodies of George Burroughs & George Jacobs, sworn by Edward Welch, William Gill, Zeb. Hill, Tom Flint, Tom West, Sam Morgan and John Bare, Jurats." *Mass Archives,* 1692; Peabody Essex Museum, Salem, MA.

Spectral Evidence

The Salem Trials were controversial from the beginning. Chief Justice Stoughton and the eight Judges of the Court of Oyer Et Terminer were following the English laws of that time. The accused received no legal assistance, had no defense lawyers or witnesses to speak at court on their behalf. Being accused was itself a sign of guilt and prisoners were presumed guilty until proven innocent.

First there was the swearing out of one or more formal complaints with the local magistrate against someone for certain acts of witchcraft. Then a warrant was issued specifying the date and place the accused was required to appear for Examination or preliminary hearing. The local constable then brought the accused under arrest to their Examination, where it would be determined whether or not there was enough evidence for a formal trial. If accusations included testimony that the prisoner had made a covenant with the Devil, then the alleged witch was turned over by the Essex County authorities for imprisonment to await trial by the Court of Oyer Et Terminer.

For a conviction of witchcraft, the judges looked for the report of those appointed to search the body of the accused for "witchmarks." The suspect's ability to perform feats of super strength represented other evidence. Observing the reactions of the Afflicted Girls when faced with the accused in court, offered further proof of guilt, along with the testimonies of those who were convinced that they had suffered injury or loss of property due to the witch's powers.

Most controversial among ministers, magistrates, and citizens throughout the Salem Trials was spectral evidence, based on the belief that the Devil could not take the shape of a human being without that person's permission. It was this decision of the Court of Oyer Et Terminer to allow it for witchcraft convictions, based upon former witchcraft trials in England, which led to the twenty executions of 1692. This meant if your specter or spirit had been observed causing harm to a victim, even if only in someone's dream, this was proof of witchcraft, since only someone working for the Devil could send his spirit to torment innocent people. There was no possible defense against a witness who told the court that your shape had hurt them even though you were locked up in jail at that time.

"A Dreadful Knot of Witches"

The Smallest Witch

They spare not even infancy: poor little Dorcas Good,
The vagrant's child-but four years old!
Who says that baby could
To Satan sign her soul away
condemns this business blind,
As but the senseless babbling of a weak and wicked mind.

— Lucy Larcom in "Mistress Hale of Beverly."

Several weeks after Sarah Good was imprisoned, her four year old daughter, Dorcas, was arrested. The Afflicted Girls claimed that the little girl's specter had attacked them in revenge for their having accused her mother, and the authorities found marks on their arms that seemed to resemble the bites of a child.

Little Dorcas needed little urging from the magistrates when it came to calling her mother a witch. Had not her own father failed to provide support for them so that they were made to beg food from door to door in Salem Village just to stay alive?

"I may say with tears that my wife is an enemy to all good," William Good said at his wife's examination. He said that he was afraid she was either a witch or would be one very quickly!

So, when ministers and magistrates questioned the child in jail, little Dorcas told them that, yes, her mother had familiars: "... birds — one black and one yellow, that she used to hurt the afflicted persons."

When asked if she herself had any familiars, little Dorcas told them that she had a snake which sucked her fingers and the magistrates "observed a deep red spot, the bigness of a flea bite" between her tiny fingers. No, she said, the devil hadn't given her the snake. Her mother had.

If such a small child could be a confessed witch, then the Devil's hold on their Colony was even stronger than they had imagined.

Dorcas soon joined her mother in jail, where several months later, Sarah Good gave birth to a baby, who soon died. Sarah was hanged for witchcraft on July 19.

In May, on complaint of the Afflicted Girls that the accused prisoners's specters continued to torture them, all prisoners were shackled in leg irons. Before her imprisonment, the Rev. Deodat Lawson noted that Dorcas Good "looked as hale and well as other children."

On September 13, 1710, Dorcas' father, William Good, petitioned the General Court on behalf of what his family had suffered.

1. My wife Sarah Good was in prison about four months and then executed.

2. A suckling child died in prison before the mother's execution.

3. A child of four or five years old was in prison seven or eight months, and being chained in the dungeon was so hardly used and terrified that she hath ever since been very chargeable having little or no reason to govern herself. And I leave it unto the honorable Court to judge what damage I have sustained by such a destruction of my poor family.

Historical sources tell us that Dorcas Good never recovered from this terrible emotional toll from her mother's execution, her own conviction for witchcraft, and those many months in prison.

The Man of Iron

Giles Cory was a wizard strong.
A stubborn wretch was he;
And fit was he to hang on high
Upon the locust tree.

So, when before the magistrates
For trial he did come,
He would no true confession make
But was completely dumb.

"Giles Cory," said the Magistrate,
"What have you here to plead?
To these who now accuse thy soul
Of crime and horrid deed?"

Giles Cory he said not a word,
No single word spoke he.
"Giles Cory," said the Magistrate,
"We'll press it out of thee."

They got them then a heavy beam,
They laid it on his chest;
They loaded it with heavy stones,
And hard upon him prest.

"More weight!" now said this wretched man;
"More weight!" again he cried;
And he did no confession make,
But wickedly he died.

This anonymous poem, believed to have been written in the mid-nineteenth century, is a memorial to eighty-year-old Giles Corey, the only person in American history known to have been legally pressed to death.

Giles Corey was known for his terrible temper. He had already been to court several times regarding his quarrels with John Proctor and it was said he once beat a servant to death.

He firmly believed in witches and had attended the Examinations of those first accused. He even testified against his own wife, Martha. Later, when he realized his testimony had helped convict her of witchcraft, he said that she was no more guilty than he was but when he then proceeded to criticize the Afflicted Girls, they immediately cried out against him.

Following his arrest on April 19, the Afflicted Girls were so affected "with fits and troubled with pinches" that the Court ordered Giles' hands tied. Other accused witches claimed Giles was among Satan's coven plotting to destroy the church. Anne Putnam, Jr. said that his specter had appeared before her with a large book which he had ordered her to sign. When she refused, he had beaten her and kept coming after her with his Devil's book. Anne said that the specter of Giles Corey continued to torment her even after he was in prison, and choked her until she thought he would kill her.

Benjamin Gould claimed that both Giles and Martha Corey had visited his bedside and stared at him. After they left, he noticed two bruises on his side that had not been there before. And even though they were both in prison, Gould claimed he had met Giles Corey and John Proctor who, he said, had caused his foot to hurt so much that he could not put on a boot for three days.

Under English law, a defendant had three chances to plead. A person who refused to answer could not be tried in court. Giles Corey's death represented a protest against the Court. The legal term for his treatment was *Peine Forte et Dure* or "punishment strong and hard." They staked him to the ground, under a plank upon which heavy stones were placed. Then they continued to increase the weight until he either testified or died.

Mather's The Wonders of the Invisible World *strongly defended the Salem judges at a time when others were critizing them for their management of the trials.*

Cotton Mather 1665-1729

Like everyone else who lived in New England during the
17th century, the Rev. Cotton Mather believed in witches and
devils. Although he was barely 30 in 1692, he had already
established a reputation as a scholar, historian, and Puritan
church leader.

The eldest son of the Rev. Increase Mather, who was the
Colony's foremost clergyman, Cotton became the youngest
student to ever enter Harvard, starting at the age of twelve.
He developed a stutter there which would have made preaching
sermons difficult, so switched his studies to medicine and
science. He conquered his speech impairment and was eventually ordained minister of the Second Church of Boston, where
he served with his father (who was often away in England on
Colony business with the Crown.)

Cotton Mather was intensely interested in the workings of
"the Invisible World" and had recently studied the demonic possession of the four Goodwin children, for which Goody Glover,
was hanged. Most Puritans thought this Irish woman was justly
executed in order to combat Satan and his conspiracy against
New England. Mather had taken one of those afflicted Goodwin
children into his home to exorcise the Devil from her by fasting
and prayer, methods he wrote about in *Memorable Providences,
Relating to Witchcrafts and Possessions* published in 1689, and
would later advise for treating the fits of those Afflicted Salem
Village girls.

Cotton Mather believed there was " Dreadful Knot of
Witches in New England."

> Now by these confessions 'tis agreed that the Devil
> has made a deadful knot of witches in the country, and
> by the help of witches has dreadfully increased that
> knot...Yea, that at witch meetings the wretches have
> proceeded so far as to concert and consult the methods

of rooting out the Christian religion from this country, and setting up instead of it perhaps a more gross Diabolism than ever the world saw before.

—The Rev. Cotton Mather, *Wonders of the Invisible World*, 1692.

The advice of both Mather ministers was sought throughout the Salem Trials and they were among the clergy who guided the magistrates to moderation and brought a quicker end to the 1692 witch-hunt. They continually warned against the use of spectral evidence in convictions and suggested lighter punishments for those found guilty of witchcraft. Cotton Mather advised the judges to be very careful when dealing with witches.

If a drop of Innocent Blood be shed, in the Prosecution of the Witchcrafts among us, how unhappy are we! ...But on the other side, if the storm of Justice do now fall only on the Heads of those guilty Witches and Wretches which have defiled our Land, How Happy!

Wonders of the Invisible World, published in 1692, was written at the request of Governor Phips to justify the magistrates' actions, since public opinion had turned against the Court proceedings. This included extracts from five witchcraft trials. Although Cotton Mather did not attend any of the trials, he publicly defended the Court's verdicts at the one execution he did attend on August 19. He also warned of "An Horrible Plot against this Land by Witchcraft and a foundation of Witchcraft laid forty years earlier which if not discovered, would blow up and pull down all the churches in the country."

The rulers and the ministers,
tell me, what have they done,
Through all the dreadful weeks
since this dark inquest was begun,
Save to encourage thoughtless girls
in their unhallowed ways,
And bring to an untimely end
many a good woman's days?

— Lucy Larcom in "Mistress Hale of Beverly."

The Case of Martha Corey, "Gospel Woman"

Twelve days after the two Sarahs, Good and Osborne,
had been sent to prison with Tituba, a warrant was issued for
Martha Corey, cried "Witch!" by Anne Putnam, Jr. Although
her elderly husband, Giles, had been caught up in all the community excitement of witchcraft coming to Salem Village, she
would have none of it. She denounced the entire business from
the first and had even tried to prevent her husband from attending
the hearings by taking his saddle off his horse. Martha, Giles'
third wife, was in her sixties and a member of the Rev. Samuel
Parris' church at Salem Village. As a church communicant and
among the Puritan Elect, she did not fit the witch-figure
stereotype of those first three accused.

After Goodwife Corey was cried out against, several town
leaders from her church went to young Anne Putnam to ask
what clothes Corey was wearing during her spectral visits to
her. The child replied she had been blinded and could not tell.
When they went to the Corey home later, Martha greeted the two
men saying, "I know what you have come for. You are come to
talk with me about being a witch, but I am none. I cannot help
people's talking about me." That she knew why they had come
would later be used as evidence against her.

"Goodwife Corey told us she did not think there were any
witches. We told her we were satisfied with the first three in
jail. She said we could not blame the Devil for making witches
of them, for they were idle, slothful persons and minded nothing
that was good." Her arrest, followed a few days later by that
of Rebecca Nurse, signified a religious crisis for the Colony.
If such upstanding community and church members could be
accused of witchcraft, then the Devil had the power to conquer
innocent people. No one could be trusted! Your neighbor, as
well as the person who sat beside you at the Meetinghouse,
could be a witch!

The Examination
of Rebekah Nurse at Salem village
24. Mar. 1691

Mr. Hathorn - What do you say (speaking to one afflicted) have
you seen this Woman hurt you.
Yes, she beat me this morning
Abigail Have you been hurt by this Woman
yes
Ann Putnom in a grievous fit cryed out that
she hurt her.
Goody Nurse, here are two Ann Putman. the child &
Abigail Williams complain of your hurting them
What do you say to it
N. I can say before my Eternal father I am innocent, &
god will clear my innocency

- - - - - - - - -

You do know whither you are guilty. & have familiarity
with the Devil, & now when you are here present to
see such a thing as these testify a black man whis-
pering in your ear, & birds about you what do you
say to it-
It is all false I am clear

- - - - -

Is it not an unaccountable case that when they
you are examined these persons are afflicted an
I have got no body to look to but God

John Hathorne
Janathan. Corwin

A copy of pages from the Examination of Rebecca Nurse.

"We must not believe all that these distracted children say," Martha Corey told the judges at her Examination on March 21. One witness testified that when Goodwife Corey "sometimes did bite her lip, Mercy Lewis and Elizabeth Hubbard and others of ye afflicted persons, were bitten; also when Corey pinched her fingers together, then Mercy Lewis and Elizabeth Hubbard and others were pinched." There was "extreme agony of all the afflicted." Excerpts from Martha Corey's Hearing follow:

Hathorne: You are now in the hands of authority. Tell me now why you hurt these persons.

Corey: I do not.

Hathorne: Then, who does?

Corey: Pray give me leave to go to prayer. (She requested this numerous times.)

Hathorne : We did not send for you to go to prayer. Tell me why you hurt these children.

Corey: I am an innocent person. I never had to do with witchcraft since I was born. I am a gospel woman.

Hathorne: Do you not see these complaints of you?

Corey: The Lord open the eyes of the magistrates and ministers; the Lord show this power to discover the guilty.

Hathorne: Tell us who hurts these children.

Corey: I do not know.

Hathorne: If you be guilty of this fact, do you think you can hide it?

Corey: The Lord knows.

Hathorne: Well then tell us what you know of this matter.

Corey: Why, I am a gospel woman, and do you think I can have to do with witchcraft too?

Hathorne: How could you tell, then, that the child was bid to observe what clothes you wore when some came to speak with you? You dare to lie in this assembly? You are now before authority. I expect the truth.

Martha Corey was committed for trial and faced Court at its September sitting, where she was convicted. She was executed on September 22. Like her fellow Salem Village church member, Rebecca Nurse, she was excommunicated and, according to Puritan belief, thus lost hope for eternal salvation.

"Martha Corey, wife of Giles Corey, protesting her innocency, concluded her life with an eminent prayer upon the ladder to the gallows."

— Robert Calef, *More Wonders of the Invisible World*, London, 1700.

John Proctor's Letter From Prison

The arrest of John Proctor, the upstanding citizen and farmer of Salem Farms, (now Peabody) Massachusetts, marked another turning point in the trials. He was the first man to be indicted, had openly criticized the trials and the Court's methods, and had little patience for the hysterical antics of those Afflicted Girls of Salem Village. One of them, Mary Warren, was a servant in his own household. He'd put her to the spinning wheel, warning her that if she got up, he would whip her. That stopped her fits.

The day after Rebecca Nurse's Examination, Proctor went to Salem Village "to fetch home his jade... If we let those girls go unchecked, we should all be branded devils and witches quickly. They should rather be put to the whipping post!" He threatened to thrash the devil out of Mary Warren.

Four days after the execution of Goody Nurse and others accused of witchcraft, he told his maidservant, "If you are afflicted, I wish you were more afflicted." Indeed, he wished all the Afflicted persons were worse afflicted.

"Master, what makes you say so?" Mary Warren asked.

"Because you go to bring out innocent persons," Proctor replied.

His wife, Elizabeth Proctor, was arrested on April 11. He accompanied her to her court hearing, which was recorded by Samuel Sewall in his *Diary:*

> Went to Salem, where, in the Meeting House, the persons accused of witchcraft were examined; was a very great assembly; 'Twas awful to see how the afflicted persons were agitated.

While defending his wife against the accusations, John Proctor was himself cried out against by the Afflicted Girls as "a most dreadful wizard."

On August 5, the Proctors faced trial together before the Court of Oyer & Terminer, where they were both condemned to death on charges of witchcraft. His wife escaped the gallows because she was expecting a child. Soon after Proctor's arrest, court deputies went to his farm where they seized all his "goods, provisions, and livestock, selling the cattle or slaughtering them to ship to the West Indies. The officers even emptied beer from a barrel and soup from a pot in order to take away the pot, leaving nothing in the house for the support of the Proctor children." (R. Calef, *More Wonders*, 1700).

Their oldest children, William and Sarah Proctor, were also arrested and imprisoned on charges of witchcraft.

> William, when he was examined, because he would not confess that he was guilty, when he was innocent, they tied him neck and heels until the blood gushed out at his nose, and would have kept him so 24 hours, if someone more merciful than the rest, had not taken pity on him, and caused him to be unbound.

In this letter to the clergy written from prison, John Proctor likened such treatment to the methods of the Spanish Inquisition.

Thirty-one of Proctor's former neighbors at Ipswich signed a petition on his behalf and twenty friends from Salem submitted another petition to the Court in an attempt to save his life, attesting to the family's faultless life and excellent character:

> ...we Judge them innocent of the Crime...having several years known John Proctor and his wife, do testify that we have never heard that they were ever suspected to be guilty of the crime now charged upon them, and several of us being their near neighbors do testify that to they lived Christian lives in their family and were ever ready to help such as stood in need of their help.

The petitions did little to help the Proctors. After the executions of July 19, John Proctor realized he could not receive a fair trial in Essex County, so on July 23rd, two weeks before his own trial was scheduled, he wrote a letter from prison to the leading Boston ministers, in which he requested a change in government policy and asked for clerical leadership. The five clerymen to whom he addressed his letter were members of a committee appointed by Governor Phips to set up guidelines for the Court of Oyer and Terminer. He claimed that the accused had been condemned "already before our trials" and asked that the trials be moved to Boston or that the clergy might bring a change in magistrates "bringing in some who would not heed the hysterical fits of girls." He asked that some ministers be present at the trials, "hoping thereby you may be the means of saving the shedding of innocent blood...we know, in our own consciences, we are all innocent persons."

Proctor also wrote of the plight or his fellow prisoners, including the torture done upon his son as well as upon the sons of Martha Carrier.

Acting upon this letter to the clergy, the Rev. Increase Mather and seven other ministers met in Cambridge on August 1 to take up the question of prejudgment addressed by Proctor from prison. They concurred that "the devil may sometimes represent an

innocent person as tormenting such as are under diabolical influ-
ences, though such things are rare and extraordinary." It was the
old, continuing argument of spectral evidence allowed as court
testimony and it could not save John Proctor.

At Proctor's execution the Rev. Nicholas Noyes refused his
request for time to prepare by prayer "because he would not
own himself to be a witch." When he was hanged on August 19,
Thomas Brattle wrote that they said "they wished their blood
might be the last innocent blood shed...With great emotion, they
entreated Mr. Cotton Mather to pray with them. They prayed
that God would discover what witchcrafts were among us; they
forgave their accusers; they spoke without reflection on Jury and
Judges...and seemed to be very sincere, upright, and sensible of
their circumstances...especially Proctor and Willard, whose
whole management of themselves, from Gaol to Gallows and
whilst at the Gallows, was very affecting and melting to the
hearts of some considerable Spectators." (Thomas Brattle,
Letter of October 8, 1692)

Mary Easty's Petition From Prison

The belief that witchcraft ran in families is well demonstrated
by the cases of the three Towne sisters whose mother, Joanna
Blessing Towne, had been accused of being a witch many years
before. Rebecca Nurse, Sarah Cloyce, and Mary Easty were
all accused and convicted. Only Goody Cloyce escaped the
hangman's noose.

These sisters were pious and respected members of church
and community, but their male relatives were known to support
the faction against the Putnam family and did not support Mr.
Parris' ministry at Salem Village. Mary's husband, Issac Easty,
had argued over land with some of those same Salem Village
men who championed the Rev. Samuel Parris' cause.

Mary Easty and her husband, who was a successful farmer in Topsfield, had raised seven children. Her two sisters had already been accused of witchcraft and were in jail when she was arrested April 21. A number of the Afflicted Girls went into fits when Mary Easty was brought into the courtroom. Asked by Judge Hathorne if the prisoner was hurting them, they were unable to reply because Goody Easty's specter would not permit them to speak.

Judge Hathorne: What have you done to these children?

Mary Easty: I know nothing of it.

Hathorne: How can you say you know nothing when you see these tormented and they accuse you?"

Easty: Would you have me accuse myself?

Hathorne: Yes, if you be guilty. How far have you complied with Satan whereby he take?

Easty: Sir, I have never gone with Satan, but have prayed against him all my days. What would you have me do?

Hathorne: Confess, if you are guilty.

Easty: I will say it (again) I am clear of this sin."

Hathorne: Of what sin?

Easty: Of witchcraft.

She sounded so sincere that Hathorne had to ask the girls again, "Are you sure this is the woman?"

In her nervousness, Mary Easty had clasped her hands together, a gesture that was followed by the locking together of Mercy Lewis' hands, supposedly caused by Mary's specter.

Hathorne: Look now, Goodwife Easty, your hands are open and the girl's hands are open.

When Mary Easty bowed her head, the girls' heads were then forced down so low that they feared their necks would snap. "Straighten out her head or our necks will break!" they cried out.

When she could finally speak again, twelve year old Anne Putnam cried, "Oh Goody Easty, Goody Easty, you are the woman! You are the woman!"

Hathorne: What did you think about all this before your sisters were accused? Did you think it was witchcraft?"

Easty: I cannot tell you.

Hathorne: Why, don't you think it is witchcraft?"

Easty: It is an evil spirit, but whether it's witchcraft, I do not know.

While Mary was in jail, a group of her friends met with the magistrates on her behalf and convinced them to release her. All the Afflicted Girls except Mercy Lewis dropped charges, but when Goody Easty was freed, Mercy suffered fits for several days until the other girls also cried out against Mary Easty. She was arrested again.

Mercy Lewis, Mary Walcott, Elizabeth Hubbard, Abigail Williams, and Anne Putnam, Jr. were overcome with such agonizing seizures when Mary Easty was brought into Court that the Rev. Hale had to lead them in prayer. For the second time Goody Easty was committed to jail, where she was reunited with her sisters. Later, she and Sarah Cloyce wrote a petition to the court requesting legal counsel. They also asked that character witnesses be permitted to testify on their behalf. They did not think the testimony of Afflicted Persons should be used against the defendants unless there was other legal evidence. The Petition of the two sisters was either denied or ignored.

On September 13, shortly before her execution, Mary Easty wrote a Petition to the "honorable judge and bench now sitting in judicature in Salem and the reverend ministers." In it she pleaded for others who had been unjustly accused and expressed hope that they might be spared her fate.

> I petition to your honors not for my own life, for
> I know I must die, and my appointed time is set. But
> the Lord He knows it is, if it be possible, that no more
> innocent blood may be shed, which undoubtedly cannot
> be avoided in the way and course you go in... by my own
> innocency, I know you are in the wrong way... I would
> humbly beg of you that your Honors would be pleased
> to examine these afflicted persons strictly, and keep them
> apart some time, and likewise to examine some of these
> confessing witches, I being confident there is several of
> them have belied themselves and others, as will appear,
> if not in this world, I am sure in the world to come
> whither I am going.
>
> The Lord alone, who is the searcher of all hearts,
> knows that I shall answer it at the Tribunal Seat that I
> know not the least thing of witchcraft, therefore I cannot,
> I durst not, belie my own soul. I beg your honors not to
> deny this my humble petition for a poor dying innocent
> person...
>
> — Paul Boyer & Stephen Nissenbaum, eds. *Salem Witchcraft
> Papers*, (New York: De Capo Press, 1977), pp. 303-304.

Although the authorities took no action on this document, Mary Easty's Petition forced them to reevaluate the witchcraft persecutions and helped bring the trials to an end. Goodwife Easty did not doubt that witches existed. However, she believed that many of those who had confessed to witchcraft had done so to save their lives and were not guilty. She understood that she could have saved herself by pretending to have signed the Devil's book but she was not willing to lie.

When she took her last farewell of her husband, children, and friends, was, as is reported by them present, as Serious, Religious, Distinct, and Affectionate as could well be exprest, drawing tears from the eyes of almost all present."

— Robert Calef, *More Wonders of the Invisible World*, London, 1700.

Mary Easty was executed on September 22, along with Giles Corey's wife, Martha, Alice Parker, Ann Pudeator, Margaret Scott, Wilmont "Mammy" Redd, and Mary Parker and Samuel Wardwell of Andover.

"What a sad thing, the Rev. Nicholas Noyes said from astride his horse, "to see eight Firebrands of Hell hanging there!"

Beyond Salem Village

The Death of Goody Nurse

[July 19, 1692]

The chill New England sunshine
Lay on the kitchen floor;
The wild New England north wind
Came rattling at the door.

And by the wide old fire-place,
Deep in her cushioned chair,
Lay back an ancient woman,
With shining snow-white hair.

The peace of God was on her face,
Her eyes were sweet and calm,
And when you heard her earnest voice
It sounded like a psalm...

So weak and silent as she lay,
Her warm hands clasped in prayer,
A sudden knocking at the door
Came on her unaware.

And as she turned her hoary head,
Besside her chair there stood
Four grim and grisly Puritans-
No visitants for good.

They came upon her like a host,
And bade her speak and tell
Why she had sworn a wicked oath
To serve the powers of hell...

She glared at them with starting eyes,
Her voice essayed no sound;
She gasped like any hunted deer
The eager dogs surround.

"Answer us!" hoarse and loud they cry;
She looked from side to side-
No human help-"Oh gracious God!"
In agony she cried.

Then, calling back her feeble life,
The white lips uttered slow,
"I am as pure as babe unborn
From this foul thing, ye know..."

They tortured her with taunt and jeer,
They vexed her night and day-
No husband's arm nor sister's tears
Availed their rage to stay...

They fastened chains about her feet,
And carried her away;
For many days in Salem jail
Alone and ill she lay...

At last the prison door stood wide,
They led the saint abroad;
By many an old familiar place
Her trembling footsteps trod.

Till faint with weakness and distress,
She climbed a hillside bleak,
And faced the gallows built thereon,
Still undisturbed and meek.

They hanged this weary woman there,
Like any felon stout;
Her white hairs on the cruel rope
Were scattered all about...

A woman old and innocent,
To die a death of shame,
With kindred, neighbors, friends thereby,
And none to utter blame.

Oh God, that such a thing should be
On earth which Thou hast made!
A voice from heaven answered me,
"Father forgive," He said.

— Rose Terry Cooke, *Poems of American History,* Burton Egbert Stevenson, ed. (N.Y.: Houghton Mifflin, 1963) pp. 90-91.

The Tall Man From Boston

Seventy-year-old John Alden was the son of the Plymouth cooper who had come over on the *Mayflower*. Although the Salem Village girls had most likely never met him, he was well-known throughout New England as a sea captain who had become rich from the fur trade. Alden is believed to be "the tall man from Boston" named by Tituba and some of the Afflicted Girls. Judge Bartholomew Gedney said he had known Captain Alden for many years and had always considered him a good man, but now "was obliged to change his opinion because when Alden touched the poor child, she came out of her fit." As for Captain Alden, he had no use for the touch-test:

> I cannot but condemn this method of the Justices, of making this touch of the hand a rule to discover witchcraft because I am fully persuaded that it is a superstitious method...

After fifteen weeks in prison, John Alden escaped to New York. He did not return to Boston until April of 1693, when he was cleared of all charges. He wrote an account of his arrest and treatment, an excerpt of which follows:

> John Aldin Senior, of Boston, in the County of Suffolk, Mariner, on the 28th Day of May, 1692, was sent for by the Magistrates of Salem, in the County of Essex, upon the Accusation of a company of poor distracted, or possessed Creatures or Witches; and being sent by Mr. Stoughton, arrived there the 31st of May, and appeared at Salem-village, before Mr. Gidney, Mr. Hathorn, and Mr. Corwin.
>
> Those Wenches being present, who played their jugling tricks, falling down, crying out, and staring in Peoples' Faces; the Magistrates demanded of them several times, who it was of all the People in the Room that hurt them? one of these Accusers pointed several times at one Captain Hill, there present, but spake nothing; the same Accuser had a Man standing at her

back to hold her up; he stooped down to her Ear, then she cried out, Alden, Alen afflicted her; one of the Magistrates asked her if she had ever seen Alden. She answered no, he asked her how she knew it was Alden? She said, the Man told her so.

Then all were ordered to go down into the Street, where a Ring was made; and the same Accuser cried out, "there stands Alden, a bold fellow with his Hat on before the Judges, he sells Powder and Shot to the Indians and French, and lies with the Indian Squaes, and has Indian Papooses." Then was Alden commited to the Marshal's Custody, and his Sword taken from him; for they said he afflicted them with his Sword. After some hours Alden was sent for to the Meetinghouse in the Village before the Magistrates; who required Alden to stand upon a Chair, to the open view of all the People...

... They bid Alden look upon the Accusers, which he did, and then they fell down. Alden asked Mr. Gidney, what Reason there could be given, why Alden's looking upon *him* did not strike *him* down as well; but no reason was given that I heard...Alden told Mr. Gidney, that he could assure him that there was a lying Spirit in them, for I can assure you that there is not a word of truth in all these say of me.

Pact With the Devil For Protection
Against the Native Americans

Mary Toothaker was terrified of Indians. Violent border raids were becoming increasingly frequent in isolated New England villages. Indeed, while she was in Salem Prison another war party attacked her hometown of Billerica, killing six people. A few days later, they returned to torch the Toothaker's own farm. The Toothakers had seven children and times were hard. Since her husband had been Warned Out of Billerica for medical malpractice and had been residing on the North Shore, Mary had been receiving charity from the town and two of their children had been bound out to local families. Her twenty-two year old son, Allen, who was still recovering from battle wounds sustained fighting the French and Indians, lived in Andover.

Mary's husband, Dr. Roger Toothaker, was already in the Boston jail on charges of witchcraft when she and her nine-year old daughter, Margaret, were taken into custody on May 28, the same day that her sister, Martha Carrier, was arrested at Andover. Mary was accused of afflicting Mercy Lewis, Anne Putnam, Mary Walcott, Abigail Williams, and others. At her *Examination* Mary Toothaker confessed to making a pact with the Devil because he promised her protection against the Indians.

> After many questions and negative answers were returned and her striking down of several of the Afflicted Persons with her looks, she desired to tell the truth. She said this May last she was under great discontentedness and troubled with fear about the Indians and used often to dream about fighting with them...she had often prayed but thought she was the worse for praying and knows not but that the Devil tempted her not to pray...she went in her Spirit to Timothy Swan's and did often think of him & her hands would be clinched, and she would grip the dishcloth...and so think of the person...the Devil appeared to her in the shape of a Tawny man and promised to keep her from the Indians and she should have happy days...

— Excerpt from *Examination & Confession of Widow Toothaker,* February 1, Verdict of "Not Guilty" 932-933. See also Boyer & Nissenbaum, *Salem Witchcraft Papers* (N.Y.: Da Capo Press, 1977) pp. 767-769.

"Rebellion is As the Sin of Witchcraft"

Everyone had a place in Puritan society, according to God's Plan. Success was a sign of God's favor and wealth was measured mostly by the amount of land a man owned. According to the Puritans, God had preordained some men to positions of wealth, status, and leadership. Others, He had deemed servants to remain lower in the social order. Wives were expected to be subservient to their husbands, as servants and apprentices were to follow their masters' commands. Children had to obey their parents just as citizens must defer to their ministers and magistrates. The whole structure of 17th century Massachusetts depended upon maintaining this hierarchy.

Those who complained about their lot in life were believed to be more easily tempted by Satan and his agents, who promised them material goods and a better life if they would do work for him on earth. "The Devil loves to fish in troubled waters," the Rev. Cotton Mather said.

Fourteen-year-old William Barker Jr. was arrested for afflicting Andover teenagers Martha Sprague, Abigail Martin and Rose Foster. Like his father, he confessed, although he said he had only been in "the snare of the Devil six days."

The "World had gone hard" for forty-seven year old William Barker Sr. of Andover "being a poor man, having a great family" he had signed the Devil's Book since Satan promised to pay all his debts and he should live comfortably." (Confession of William Barker, Sr., August 29, 1692) As he went to the woods to fetch his cow, he had "come upon the shape of a black dog which looked very fiercely upon him."

Barker's *Confession* hinted at a society in which "all men would be created equal" and be provided with the opportunity for "pursuit of happiness,"a political philosophy unimaginable to Puritans living in Massachusetts Bay Colony in the 1690s.

The Devil promised that all his people should live bravely; all should be equal; there should be no day of resurrection nor of Judgment, and neither punishment nor shame for sin.

Barker said he'd been at a meeting of witches in Salem Village with the Rev. George Burroughs (who had already been executed). Satan's design, Barker explained, was to abolish all the churches in the country and set up his own worship. There were already 307 witches here..."who are much disturbed with the Afflicted Persons because they are discovered by them." (Boyer & Nissenbaum, ed. *Salem Witchcraft Papers* I, p. 67-68).

Andover's Touch Test

By summer the Afflicted girls were famous. The doctors could not tell what was the matter with Joseph Ballard's wife who had been sick so long in Andover. Hearing about the Salem Trials, he suspected witchcraft, so he rode to Salem Village to fetch Anne Putnam and Mary Wolcott to see if they could help. They were taken to Goodwife Ballard and to other Andover sickbeds for some claimed "there were more than forty who could raise the Devil at Andover." Indeed, more would be accused of witchcraft from this town than from any other in Essex County, and Andover had its own circle of teenage accusers who were Afflicted.

Some forty warrants were signed by local magistrate, Dudley Bradstreet, and when he refused to sign any more, he and his wife were cried out against.

Although it was unlikely that the Salem Village girls knew the names of those accused from Andover, more arrests followed a town Touch Test. Citizens gathered at the Meetinghouse where those suspected of witchcraft were blindfolded, while the Afflicted were in their fits and led to each hysterical girl to be touched. Since it was believed that such torments could be stopped by a witch's touch, calming the hysterical meant immediate arrest on suspicion of witchcraft.

Andover would also have the greatest number of confessed witches, as well as the most children arrested. Following the hangings of July 19, it had become clear that the only persons executed were those who claimed they were not guilty. The magistrates, ever determined to uncover Satan's plot to destroy their Colony, kept the confessing "witches" in jail unchained so they could keep badgering these confessors to provide them with names of others in league with Satan.

"Queen of Hell"

When Martha Carrier and her family moved from Billerica back to her parent's home in Andover in 1689, they brought smallpox with them. Although smallpox epidemics were not unusual occurences throughout the 17th century, this town had thus been spared its scourge. Susannah Sheldon's testimony, "I see the souls of thirteen murdered by Goody Carrier at Andover," would directly relate to this epidemic.

Martha Carrier was warned-off by the Andover selectmen: "for spreading smallpox with wicked carelessness...smitten with some of her children with that contagious disease..." She was banned from the Meetinghouse. Not only did she refuse to leave Andover, she insisted that the town support her family during their illness.

There was no lack of evidence against Martha Carrier. Not only did her neighbors testify against her, so did her own children. At her *Examination* five Afflicted Girls "fell into the most intolerable cries and agonies," claiming they were being stuck with pins. Excerpts follow:

Judge: Susannah Sheldon, who hurts you?

Answer: Goody Carrier, she bites me, pinches me, and tells me she would cut my throat if I did not sign her book.

Judge: What do you say to this you are charged with?

Carrier: I have not done it.

Judge: Can you look upon these (girls and not knock them down?)

Carrier: They will disassemble if I look upon them.

Judge: You see you look upon them and they fall down.

Carrier: It is false. The Devil is a liar.

Mary Walcott then saw the ghosts of the thirteen people murdered by Martha Carrier. Carrier's specter had supposedly twisted the girls' necks all the way around. Susannah Sheldon's hands were tied together with a wheelband by Goody Carrier's specter.

Carrier (to Judges): It is a shameful thing that you should mind these folks that are out of their wits.

Judge: Do you not see them?

Carrier: It's no matter if their necks are twisted off. If I speak you will not believe me.

Judge: You do see them suffering.

Carrier: You lie. I am wronged!

"The tortures of the afflicted were so great that there was no enduring of it, so that Carrier was ordered away to be bound hand and foot ...the manacles to keep her specter from wandering. As soon as Goody Carrier was well bound, they all had strange and sudden ease. Mary Walcott told the magistrates that this woman told her she had been a witch these forty years."

Although Andover's senior minister, Francis Dane, said she was a "victim of malicious gossip...and that there was suspicion of Goodwife Carrier among some of us before she was apprehended..." she was accused of malefic witchcraft and blamed for inflicting pain and destroying property. One of Andover's confessed witches said that the Devil promised Carrier that she would be Queen of Hell. (*Confession* of Mary Lacey, Jr.)

Allen Toothaker, Martha Carrier's nephew, claimed he lost a three year old heifer, next a yearling and then a cow and did not know any natural causes for their deaths... "but I always feared it hath been the effect of my Auint Carrier's malice." Then he'd had an argument with his cousin, Richard Carrier, who pulled him down by his hair. When he rose to strike back, he "fell down flat on the ground and had no power to stir hand or foot..." Then he "saw the shape of Martha Carrier go off his breast, and he could get up." Allen had a wound from the Indian wars four inches deep, which his Aunt Carrier told him would never be cured. Yet after her arrest, it immediately healed.

Four of Goody Carrier's neighbors testified she cast spells on their cattle. Benjamin Abbot told the Court they'd argued over some land and when he surveyed it, she lost her temper and said she "would stick as close to him as the bark on a tree and he should repent of it afore seven years came to an end. She told him she would hold his nose as close to the grindstone as ever it was held since his name was Abbot."

Soon after these threats, he suffered severe side pains; his foot swelled so that he could not walk. Dr. Prescott lanced the poison from his foot over a six week period, but then more boils appeared on his body and he hovered between life and death until the day Martha Carrier was taken into custody. As soon as she was in chains Abbot made a miraculous recovery.

The Confession of Sarah Carrier

Four of Martha Carrier's children, ranging in age from seven and a half to eighteen, were arrested on suspicion of witchcraft and imprisoned with their mother. According to John Proctor's *Letter* her teenage sons had to be tortured before they would testify that their mother had made them serve the Devil.

Sarah Carrier was examined by the magistrates on August 11:

Question:: How long have you been a witch?

Answer: Ever since I was six years old.

Q.: And how old are you now?

A..: Near eight years old, brother Richard says. I shall be eight years old November next.

Q.: Who made you a witch?

A..: My mother. She made me set my hand to a book.

Q.: How did you set your hand to it?

A..: I touched it with my fingers and the book was red, the paper of it was white. I did it in Andrew Foster's pasture and Elizabeth Johnson junior was there. So was my Aunt Toothaker and cousin Margaret.

Q.: What did they promise to give you?

A.: A black dog.

Q.: Did the dog ever come to you?

A.: No, but I saw a cat once.

Q.: What did the cat say to you?

A..: It said it would tear me in pieces if I would not set my hand to the book. My mother baptized me. The devil was not there. My mother said when she baptized me "thou are mine forever and ever and amen."

Q.: How did you afflict folks?

A..: I pinched them. I did not have poppets, but I went to them that I afflicted. I went to them in my spirit, no my body. My mother carried me around to afflict.

Q.: How did your mother carry you when she was in prison?

A..: She came like a black cat.

Q.: How did you know that it was your mother?

A..: The cat told me so. I afflicted Phelp's child last Saturday and Elizabeth Johnson joined me to do it. She had a wooden spear, about as long as her finger and she had it from the Devil. But I never did go to the witch meeting at the village.

Mary Osgood's Confession

The respected wife of a church deacon and Colonel in the militia, Mary Clements Osgood was arrested September 7 at Andover's Touch Test.. Her *Examination* and *Confession* were particularly dramatic. She said she must have become a witch about eleven years ago when she had her last child and was in a depressed state. She thought it was a real cat that she'd seen in the orchard but then, the cat had made her pray to the Devil instead of God. The Devil had presented her with a book upon which she'd put her finger and it left a red spot. She had taken midnight rides though the air with Deacon Frye's wife, Ebenezer Barker's wife, and Goodwife Tyler to Five-mile Pond, where she was baptised by the Devil. He told her she must be his, soul and body, forever, and promise to serve him. She had expected to find great satisfaction in the Devil's service but he had never given it to her and she was miserable. In company with Goody Parker, Goody Tyler, and Goody Dane, she met at Moses Tyler's house to afflict and she and Goody Dane carried the shape of Mr. Dane, the minister, between them to make people believe he had been afflicted.

About six weeks later, the Rev. Increase Mather visited Mary Osgood in prison where she told him that the *Confession* she made was wholly false. She had never touched the Devil's book, was never baptised by the Devil, and never afflicted any of her accusers nor gave consent for those afflictions. She said they told her that she would surely be hanged if she did not confess and "continued so long and so violently to urge and press her to confess that she thought verily her life would have gone from her."

Seven Andover women arrested at the Touch Test wrote about what had happened to them. Excerpts from that document follow.

> ...we knowing ourselves altogether Innocent of that Crime, we were all exceedingly astonished and amazed, and consternated and affrighted even out of our Reason; and our nearest and dearest Relations, seeing us in that dreadful condition, and knowing our great danger, apprehending there was no other way to save our lives ...but by confessing our selves...indeed that Confession that is said we made, was no other than what was suggested to us by some Gentlemen; they telling us, that we were Witches, and they knew it, and we knew it, and they knew that we knew it, which made us think that it was so; and our understanding, our reason, and our faculties almost gone, we were not capable of judging our condition; as also the hard measures they used with us, rendred us uncapable of making our Defence; but said anything and everything which they desired, and most of what we said, was but in effect a consenting to what they said. Sometime after when we were better composed, they telling of us what we had confessed, we did profess that we were Innocent, and Ignorant of such things. And we hearing that Samuel Wardwell had renounced his Confession, and quickly after Condemned and Executed, some of us were told that we were going after Wardwell.
>
> — Lt. Gov. Thomas Hutchinson, "The History of the Province of Massachusetts Bay from the Charter of King William & Mary in 1691 Until the Year 1750," Harvard College/Kraus Reprint, 1936, Chapter I.

Mary Osgood told the Rev. Increase Mather that she "wronged her conscience by confessing to witchcraft and was guilty of a great sin in belying of herself and desired to mourn for it so long as she lived."

The Fortune Teller of Andover

Samuel Wardwell of Andover in the County of Essex, Carpenter, on or about the fifteenth day of August ...and divers other days and times before as after, certain detestable arts called witchcraft and sorceries wickedly mallitiously and feloniously hath used practised and exercised...upon and against one Martha Sprague of Boxford, single woman, the day and year aforesaid and divers other days and times...is tortured, afflicted, Consumed, Pined, Wasted and Tormented and also for sundry other acts of witchcraft by the said Samuel Wardwell commited and done before and since that time against the peace of our Sovereign Lord and Lady, the King and Queen, their Crown and dignity...

— Sarah Loring Bailey, *Historical Sketches of Andover.* Boston: Houghton Mifflin/Riverside Press, 1880, pp. 210-211.

In Andover, people usually went to Carpenter Wardwell to get their fortunes told. Thomas Chandler had often heard him tell young persons their future and testified that Samuel Wardwell "was much addicted to that and made sport of it." Furthermore, he had predicted the genders of Ephraim Foster's children before they were born. Wardwell's prophecy that there would be five girls in the Foster household before a son arrived came true.

At his trial before the Court of Oyer and Terminer on September 14, Mary Walcott testified that she saw Wardwell or his specter pull Martha Sprague off the horse she was riding out of Salem and "verily believed he did it by witchcraft." (*Salem Witchcraft Papers.* III, pp. 787-788)

45

Wardwell admittted he had been "foolishly led along with the telling of fortunes which sometimes came to pass," and he used to say "The Devil take it!" when he was mad about something. The Devil may have taken advantage of that curse. Furthermore, he had the power to make animals come to him whenever he wished. Wardwell confessed to making a deal with the Devil some years back when he'd "fallen into a discontented state of mind over a maid named Barker who did not return his love." He'd seen some cats together in front of Captain Bradstreet's house. One of them assumed the form of the Devil and promised he should "live comfortably and be a captain," if he signed the book. He was baptized in the Shawsheen River "dipt all over" and renounced his former baptism.

Two week later, Samuel Wardwell recanted this *Confession* and was retried, found guilty, and nine days later, on September 22, was executed.

> Wardwell having formerly confessed himself Guilty, and after denied it, was soon brought upon his Tryal; his former Confession and Spectre Testimony was all that appeared against him. At his Execution while he was speaking to the People, protesting his Innocency, the Executioner being at the same time smoking tobacco, the smoak coming in his Face, interrupted his Discourse, those Accusers said, The Devil hindered him with smoak.

— Robert Calef, *More Wonders of the Invisible World*, London, 1700.

The accused endured many hardships and injustices. They or their families had to pay their jailers for room and board, as well as for rental of their manacles and chains. Their debts increased during their incarceration since they were unable to work at their trades or sell their crops at market. The personal property of the prisoners could be confiscated to pay jail fees.

Taken to pay the expenses of Samuel Wardwell's trial and imprisonment:

5 cows
one heifer & one yearling
9 hogs
8 loads of hay
a set of carpenter's tools
6 acres of corn upon the ground

Total Value in Pounds = 36.15

Wardwell's wife, Sarah, had also been arrested, confessed to being "in the snare of the devil six years." The Devil had promised her "clothes and the like." She signed a paper by putting her finger to it. When the magistrate asked "why she did not weep and lament for it," Sarah replied that she "could not weep." (This was a sure sign of a witch.)

Like the other confessors, Goody Wardwell described a witch meeting she had attended at Salem Village and named other witches there. A minister had also gone and "some men with pretty handsome apparel ." Sarah Wardwell spent many months in prison along with their daughter, Mercy, and a daughter-in-law, Sarah Hawkes. Sarah was one of the last three to be convicted of witchcraft under the new Superior Court of Judicature in January of 1693, but was freed a few weeks later by Governor Phips.

According to *Andover Selectmens' Records,* their four children who had been left at home all this time "were in a suffering condition " until they were finally "bound out to good and honest families." William, for example, was placed with Captain Samuel Frie "'til he come of the age of 1 and 20...Frie to teach him the trade of weaver."

The Tide Turns

Governor Phips' Letters to the Crown

Sir William Phips was born in 1651 on the Maine coast, one of 26 children born to the same mother. His father had been a gunsmith in Bristol, England who emigrated to raise sheep and become a ship's carpenter. William learned to read and write at the age of 22 in Boston, then served as master of a ship. He gained a fortune in the West Indies recovering sunken treasure from Spanish galleons, filling the Crown's coffers for which he was knighted and, in 1688, made High Sheriff of New England. He was a military hero and leader of the expedition that conquered Nova Scotia and was sent on another attack against the French in Quebec. He had no experience at government affairs, so depended on William Stoughton, whom he named Acting Governor of the Bay Colony and put in charge of the Court of Oyer Et Terminer, while he left for Maine to fight the French and their Native American allies. Excerpt from Phips' Letters to the Crown:

> ...when I came home I found many persons in a strange ferment of dissatisfaction...I found that the Devil had taken upon him the name and shape of several persons who were doubtless innocent and to my certain knowledge of good reputation for which cause I have now forbidden the committing of any more that shall be accused without unavoidable necessity, and those that have been committed I would shelter from any Proceedings against them wherein there may be the least suspicion of any wrong to be done unto the Innocent...I hereby declare that as soon as I came from fighting against their Majesties Enemyes and understood what danger some of their innocent subjects might be exposed to, if the evidence of the afflicter persons only did prevail...
> I did before any application was made unto me about it

put a stop to the procedings of the Court and they are now stopped till their Majesties pleasure be known...

In another letter, dated February 21, Phips writes:

...when I returned I found people much dissatisfied at the proceedings of the Court, for about Twenty persons were condemned and executed of which number some were thought by many persons to be innocent. The Court still proceeded in the same method of trying them, which was by the evidence of the afflicted persons who when they were brought into the Court as soon as the suspected witches looked upon them instantly fell to the ground in strange agonies and grievous torments, but when touched by them upon the arm or some other part of their flesh they immediately revived and came to themselves, upon (which) they made oath that the Prisoner at the Bar did afflict them and that they saw their shape or spectre come from their bodies which put them to such paines and torments: When I enquired into the matter I was enformed by the Judges that they begun with this, but had humane testimony against such as were condemned and undoubted proof of their being witches, but at length I found that the Devill did take upon him the shape of Innocent persons and some were accused of whose innocency I was well assured and many considerable persons of unblameable life and conversation were cried out upon as witches and wizards. The Deputy Governor notwithstanding persisted vigorously in the same method, to the great dissatisfaction and disturbance of the people, until I put an end to the Court and stopped the proceedings... When I put an end to the Court there were at least fifty persons in prison in great misery by reason of the extream cold and their poverty, most of them having only spectre evidence against them...I caused some of them to be lett out upon bayle and put the Judges upon considering of a way to relieve others and prevent them from perishing in prison, upon which some of them were convinced and acknowledged that their former proceedings were too violent and not grounded upon a right foundation but that if they might sit again, they would proceed after another method...

Salem Trials Brought to an End

Public opposition against Court proceedings increased as more and more citizens and clergy were speaking out. On October 3, fourteen ministers gathered to reexamine the legal and moral basis of the Salem Trials and to dispute the validity of spectral evidence as a determination of guilt. They decided that the Court had accused and executed innocent people and they aimed to put a stop to the witchcraft proceedings. The ministers asked the Rev. Increase Mather to write their views on these "unjustifiable means of discovering Witchcrafts" in order to prevent the taking of any wrong steps in this dark way." The result was Increase Mather's *Cases of Conscience Concerning Evil Spirits Personating Men, Witchcrafts, infallible Proofs of Guilt in such as are accused with that Crime*...published in 1693, in which he wrote:

> It were better that ten suspected witches should escape, than that one innocent person should be condemned. I had rather judge a witch to be an honest woman, than judge an honest woman as a witch.

The Rev. Increase Mather interviewed prisoners in jail, particularly the confessed witches, who later recanted. Mather had not stopped believing in witches, but he continued as he had all along, to oppose the use of spectral evidence in Court as proof of witchcraft.

The bewitched young ladies had gone too far by crying out against Lady Phips, the Governor's wife, and the wife of the Rev. John Hale of Beverly, who was Judge Corwin's mother-in-law. When Governor Phips returned to Massachusetts Bay from the French and Indian Wars on the frontier, he studied the cases of all those already executed, and found that they had all been convicted on the basis of spectral evidence.

On October 18 the Governor received a letter signed by some twenty-six Andover citizens. Their senior minister, seventy-six year old Francis Dane, seems to have been one of the few people of his time who did not believe in witches and stood against the Salem Trials from the first, even as his daughters and grand-children were accused and imprisoned. An excerpt from Rev. Dane's *Letter* to the court of January 2, 1693 follows:

> I believe many innocent persons have been accused and imprisoned; ye conceit of spectral evidence as an infallible mark did too far prevail with us. Hence we so easily parted with our neighbors of an honest and good report and members in full communion; hence we so easily parted with our children when we knew nothing in their lives nor any of our neighbors to suspect them, and thus things were hurried on, hence such strange breeches in families...
>
> — Massachusetts Archives, Vol. CXXXV, p. 92.

Some 150 accused persons remained in prisons awaiting trials, many of whom expected execution. On October 15 Governor Phips dissolved the Court of Oyer Et Terminer and on November 25, the new Superior Court of Judicature was set up according to the new Royal Charter. This Court reconvened on January 3, 1693 to deal with the witchcraft cases. Fifty-two suspects were brought into Court and forty nine of the accused were declared innocent and released. Three confessed witches were found guilty but were soon pardoned by Governor Phips.

The Guilt of Innocent Blood

> We have cause to be humbled for the mistakes and errors which have been in these Colonies, in their Pro-ceedings against persons for this crime...but such was the darkness of that day. We walked in the clouds, and could not see our way.
>
> — The Rev. John Hale, *A Modest Inquiry Into the Nature of Witch-craft*, 1702.

In January of 1696, twelve jurors signed a formal apology:

We confess that we ourselves were not capable
to understand, nor able to withstand, the mysterious
delusions of the powers of darkness and Prince of the
air...We do hereby signify to all and especially to the
surviving sufferers, our deep sense of, and sorrow for,
our errors in acting on such evidence to the condemning
of any person; and do hereby declare that we justly fear
that we were sadly deluded and mistaken, for which we
are much distressed, and do humbly beg forgiveness...
and do declare we would, none of us, do such things
again, on such grounds, for the whole world.

On August 25, 1706, Anne Putnam, Jr., who of the Afflicted
Girls had been one of the most relentless of all the accusers,
stood up in the Salem Meetinghouse while the Rev. Joseph
Green, the Rev.Samuel Parris' replacement, read her formal
apology from the pulpit:

I desire to be humbled before God for that sad and
humbling Providence that befell my father's family in
the year about 'ninety-two that I, then being in my child-
hood, should by such a Providence of God be made an instrument for the accusing of several persons of a grievous
crime, whereby their lives were taken away from them,
whom now I have just grounds and good reason to believe
they were innocent persons; and that it was a great delu-
sion of Satan that deceived me in that sad time, whereby
I justly fear I have been instrumental with others, though
ignorantly and unwittingly, to bring upon myself and this
land the guilt of innocent blood; though what was said or
done by me against any person I can truly and uprightly
say before God and man, I did it not out of any anger,
malice, or ill-will to any person, for I had no such thing
aganst any of them; but what I did was ignorantly, being
deluded by Satan.
And particularly, as I was a chief instrument of
accusing Goodwife Nurse and her two sisters, I desire
to lie in the dust, and to be humble for it, in that I was a

cause, with others, of so sad a calamity to them and their families; for which cause I desire to lie in the dust, and earnestly beg forgiveness of god, and from all those unto whom I have given just cause of sorrow and offense, whose relations were taken away or accused.

Judge Samuel Sewall (1652-1730)

One of the judges at the Salem Trials, Samuel Sewall was a successful merchant, statesman, and scholar, who graduated from Harvard in 1671. The diaries he kept for fifty-six years are among the richest resources for understanding New England life during the Colonial period. He had supported the Trials until one of his Harvard friends, the Rev. George Burroughs, was executed. Judge Sewall came to believe that innocent people had been executed at Salem and when his daughter died in 1696, he took it as a sign that God was displeased with him.

Burdened with "the blame and shame of it," Sewall publicly apologized for errors in judgment made when he served on the Court of Oyer and Terminer. Sewall was reelected to Massachusetts government thirty-three times and eventually became Chief Justice of the Massachusetts Superior Court.

August 19 – Doleful Witchcraft. George Burroughts, John Willard, Jon Proctor, Martha Carrier and George Jacobs were executed at Salem, a very great number of Spectators being present. Mr. Cotton Mather was there, Mr. Sims, Hale, Noyes, Cheever, etc. All of them said they were innocent, Carrier and all. Mr Mather says they all died by a Righteous Sentence. Mr. Burroughs, by his Speech, Prayer, protestation of his Innocence, did much move unthinking persons, which occasions their speaking hardly concerning his being executed...

September 19 – About noon, at Salem, Giles Cory was press'd to death for standing Mute; much pains was used with him two days, one after another, by the Court and Capt. Gardner of Nantucket who had been of his acquaintance: but all in vain.
September 20 – Now I hear from Salem that about 18 years ago, he was suspected to have attempted and press'd a man to death, but was cleared. 'Twas not remembered till Ann Putnam was told of it by said Cory's Specter the Sabbath-day night before the Execution...

September 21 – A petition is sent to Town in behalf of Dorcas Hoar, who now confesses; Accordingly an order is sent to the Sheriff to forbear her Execution, notwithstanding her being in the Warrant to die tomorrow. This is the first condemned person who has confess'd.

October 15 – Went to Cambridge and visited Mr. Danforth, and discoursed with Him about the Witchcraft; thinks there cannot be a procedure in the Court except there be some better consent of Ministers and People...

October 26 – A Bill is sent in about calling a Fast, and Convocation of Ministers, that may be led in the right way as to the Witchcrafts. The season and manner of doing it, is such, that the Court of Oyer and Terminer count themselves thereby dismissed...

October 29 – Mr. Russell asked whether the Court of Oyer and Terminer should sit, expressing some fear of Inconvenience by its fall. Governor said it must fall...

— Excerpts from Sewall's *Diary,* 1692, Fifth Series, Vol. V. Collections MA Historical Society.

An Act to Reverse the Attainders

Even after they were released from prison, all those who had been sentenced to death remained under Attainer which meant they had no legal rights and could not even reclaim their property.

In June of 1696 Elizabeth Proctor petitioned the Court for a Reversal of Attainder to restore her civil rights. She had wished to file an appeal to contest her husband's will but because she had been convicted of witchcraft four years before, she was "dead in the law." Although Governor Phips had emptied the jails in 1693, those found guilty of the felony of witchcraft had not yet been absolved.

Abigail Dane Faulkner, daughter of Andover's senior minister, had been convicted of the crime of witchcraft and sentenced to die. She was expecting her seventh child, which is what had saved her from the gallows. Goody Faulkner spent four months in prison but after her release, was unable to regain her former rights and reputation. In 1703, she addressed the General Court:...

I am as yet suffered to live but this only as a Malefactor convicted upon record of ye most heinous crimes that mankind can be supposed to be guilty of, which besides its utter ruining and defaming my reputation... will certainly expose myself to Imminent Danger by new accusations which will thereby be the more readily believed will remain a perpetual brand of infamy upon

Regni *ANNÆ* Reginæ Decimo.

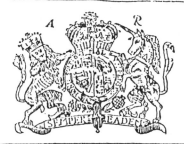

Province of the
Massachusetts-Bay.

AN ACT,

Made and Passed by the Great and General Court or
Assembly of Her Majesty's Province of the Massachusetts-
Bay in New-England, Held at Boston the 17th
Day of October, 1711. *Nathaniel Jacob Salem*

Jan. 28: 1808

An Act to Reverse the Attainders of *George Burroughs* and others for Witchcraft.

OR AS MUCH *as in the Year of our Lord One Thousand
Six Hundred Ninety Two, Several Towns within this Province were Infested with a horrible Witchcraft or Possession
of Devils ; And at a Special Court of Oyer and Terminer
holden at* Salem, *in the County of* Essex *in the same Year
One Thousand Six Hundred Ninety Two,* George Burroughs *of Wells,*
John Procter, George Jacob, John Willard, Giles Core, *and
his Wife,* Rebecca Nurse, *and* Sarah Good, *all of* Salem *aforesaid :*
Elizabeth How, *of* Ipswich, Mary Eastey, Sarah Wild *and* Abigail Hobbs *all of* Topsfield *:* Samuel Wardell, Mary Parker,
Martha Carrier, Abigail Falkner, Anne Foster, Rebecca Eames,
Mary Post, *and* Mary Lacey, *all of* Andover *:* Mary Bradbury
of Salisbury *: and* Dorcas Hoar *of* Beverly ; *Were severally Indicted, Convicted and Attainted of Witchcraft, and some of them put
to Death, Others lying still under the like Sentence of the said Court,
and liable to have the same Executed upon them.*

my family. I do humbly pray that the High and Honourable Court will please to take my case into serious consideration and order the Defacing of ye record against me, so that I may be freed from ye evil consequences thereof.

Eight years after the death of Chief Justice Stoughton, twenty-two survivors and families petitioned the General Court for reparations suffered from the loss of their relatives' lives and property. In 1711, the Attainders were reversed and some 598 pounds was paid in various amounts, to these petitioners. The Court declared their... "convictions, judgments and attainers repealed, reversed, and made null and void and that no corruption of blood or forfeitures of goods and chattels be incurred and they be reinstated in their just Credit and reputation."

In 1957, the Commonwealth of Massachusetts passed a resolution restoring the good names of the accused witches to their descendants, for the Act of Attainer had not pardoned all those accused, only the ones whose families had signed the Petition of 1704.

(*Massachusetts Resolves of 1957,* Chapter 145) the State Legislative Committee on Constitutional Law passed a bill "to reverse the attainers, judgments, and convictions for witchcraft...of all the condemned.

The Salem Witch Trials
Tercentenary Memorial

The legacy and significance of the Salem Trials is preserved
in a public art memorial adjacent to the Colonial Charter Street
Cemetery, where Judge John Hathorne and others who lived
in the town in 1692 are buried. Arthur Miller, author of "The
Crucible," unveiled the winning design which was selected
from 246 entries in an international competition. In June, 1992
Elie Wiesel, Holocaust survivor and winner of the Nobel Peace
Prize, spoke at the dedication ceremony: "...to consecrate, honor
and remember the victims. We still have our Salems," he said.
"There is one word that characterizes what happened here and
that word is fanaticism."

Designed by artist/architect team Maggie Smith and James
Cutler of Bainbridge Island, Washington, the Tercentenary
Memorial reminds us of the lessons of tolerance to be learned
from studying the Salem Witch Trials. The area is surrounded
on three sides by a granite wall and is entered by a theshold
carved with the victims' cries of innocence. Stone benches
within the memorial bear the names and dates of execution
of each of the twenty who were put to death.

Afflicted Females of Salem Village Who Were the Chief Accusers

Sarah Bibber, age 36

Elizabeth Booth, 18 years, testified in 8 cases

Sarah Churchill, 20, servant of George Jacobs, hanged as a wizard

Elizabeth Hubbard, 17, an orphan living with her uncle, Dr. Griggs (testified in 20 cases)

Mercy Lewis, 19, an orphan who saw her family slaughtered by Indians, bound-out to Thomas Putnam, Salem Village Church clerk. Previously servant in household of the Rev. George Burroughs, hanged for witchcraft. She testified in 10 cases

Elizabeth "Betty" Parris, age 9, the minister's daughter

Gertrude Pope, a middle aged woman

Ann Putnam, Sr., wife of Thomas Putnam

Anne Putnam, Jr. 12 years (testified in 19 cases)

Susannah Sheldon, 18, testified in 8 cases

Mary Walcott, 17, Thomas Putnam's niece (testified in 16 cases)

Mary Warren, 20, servant of John Proctor (hanged for witch craft); testified in 12 cases

Abigail Williams, 11, an orphan living with her uncle, the Rev. Samuel Parris; testified in 8 cases

In 1692 these girls and young women believed to be victims of Satan's possession became the most important and powerful people in town. The clergy met to discuss them and prayed over them constantly. The magistrates summoned them to Meetinghouse and before Court to name their tormenters. Adults suggested names for them to "Cry Witch" upon. Throughout the Salem Trials, they were chief witnesses for the prosecution in judicial hearings against those accused of witchcraft. By summer these young women were being invited to other Essex County towns to identify their local witches.

Although Andover first summoned the Salem Village girls to help rout out their witches, the town soon had its own circle of Afflicted, led by sixteen-year-old Martha Sprague, named a victim in twenty cases. Others were Rose Foster, Abigail Martin (a sixteen-year-old afflicted by thirteen alleged witches), twelve-year-old Phebe Chandler, and Sarah Phelps, a ten-year-old, who was afflicted by six people. Numerous Andover citizens were implicated in the sufferings of the Afflicted Girls of Salem Village.

Suggested Further Reading

Boyer, Paul, & Stephen Nissenbaum. *Salem Possessed.* The Social Origins of Witchcraft. Cambridge, MA: Harvard University, 1974.

Burr, George Lincoln, ed. *Narratives of the Witchcraft Cases 1648-1706.* Charles Scribners, 1914. (Original Narratives of Early New England History) Barnes & Noble Reprint, 1946, 1975.

Godbeer, Richard. *The Devil's Dominion;* Magic and Religion in Early New England. Cambridge University Press, 1991.

Hansen, Chadwick. *Witchcraft at Salem.* New York: G. Braziller, 1969. Reprint, New York.: Mentor Book/New American Library, 1969.

Levin, David. *What Happened In Salem?* (Contains primary documents pertaining to trials; "Young Goodman Brown," by Nathaniel Hawthorne and *A Mirror for Witches* by Esther Forbes) New York, Harcourt Brace Jovanovich, Inc., 1960.

McMillen, Persis W. *Currents of Malice* ; Mary Towne Esty and Her Family in Salem Witchcraft. Portsmouth, New Hampshire: Peter E. Randall, 1990.

Miller, Arthur. *The Crucible* : A Play in Four Acts. New York: Viking Press, 1953; Penguin Books, 1981.

Richardson, Katherine W. *The Salem Witchcraft Trials.* Salem, MA: Essex Institute, 1990.

Starkey, Marion L *The Devil in Massachusetts: A Modern Enquiry into the Salem Witch Trials.* New York: A. A. Knopf, 1949, Reprint: Garden City: Anchor Books/ Doubleday, 1969.

Trask, Richard, compiler. *Salem Village and The Witch Hysteria.* Amawalk, New York: Grossman Publ., Viking Press; Golden Owl, 1975; reprint, 1991. (Collection of facsimile documents in Jackdaw M-A16).

Reading Material For Young People

Clapp, Patricia. *Witches' Children:* A Story of Salem. New York: Lothrop, Lee & Shepard, 1982. **Y**

Cobblestone: The History Magazine for Younger People,Witchcraft Issue #1086. Peterborough, New Hampshire: Cobblestone Publisher, Inc. October, 1986. **J**

Jackson, Shirley. *The Witchcraft of Salem Village.* New York: Landmark Books, Random House, 1956. **Y**

Kent, Zachary. *Story of the Salem Witch Trials (* Cornerstones of Freedom) Chicago: Children's Press, 1986. **J**

Krensky, Stephen. *Witch Hunt:* It Happened In Salem Village. (Step Into Reading/Step 4 Book) New York: Random House, 1989. **J**

Petry, Ann. *Tituba of Salem Village.* N.Y.: New York: Thomas Y. Crowell, 1964. **Y**

Rinaldi, Ann. *A Break with Charity.* A Story of the Salem Witch Trials. N. Y.:Harcourt Brace Jovanovich, Gulliver Books, 1992. **Y**

Starkey, Marion. *The Visionary Girls*, Boston: Little Brown, 1973. **Y**

Van der Linde, Laurel. *The Devil in Salem Village;* The Story of the Salem Witchcraft Trials. (Spotlight on American History) Brookfield, CT: Millbrook Press, 1992. **J**

Woldman, Hilary Ann. *The Salem Witch Hunt,* A one-act play. Discovery Enterprises, Lowell, MA 1992. **Y**

Zeinert, Karen. *The Salem Witchcraft Trials.* N.Y.: Franklin Watts, 1989. **J**

J = Juvenile   **Y** = Youth

VHS Video Cassettes:

"Days of Judgment: The Salem Witch Trials of 1692." *Peabody Essex Museum,* 1992. (documentary).

"Three Sovereigns for Sarah," *Night Owl Productions,* 1986. (Docudrama).

Definitions

Baptism — The ceremony of admitting persons into membership in the Christian church by a sacred ceremony using water as a symbol of washing away sin. The Devil supposedly baptized witches to serve him as a perversion of Christianity.

bound-out — The legal system common in Early America of placing poor or orphaned children to board with families other than their own, where they would be fed, clothed, and taught a trade that would insure their future independence.

conspiracy — A secret plot for some political end or unlawful purpose. The Puritans of Massachusetts Bay were convinced that Satan had organized a conspiracy, using witches as his agents to overthrow their Christian Colony.

covenant — A solemn pact, promise, or pledge of faith to defend and maintain certain doctrines and policies. The Puritans had made a sacred Covenant with God to create Christian settlements in the American wilderness. They believed that every witch had made a covenant with the Devil to bring harm upon people.

execution — Witchcraft was a capital crime for which convicted witches must be executed. Witches were never burned in New England, as they had been in Europe. This Massachusetts Bay Colony law was based upon the Bible. *1641, 1648*: If any man or woman be a witch (that is hath or consulteth with a familiar spirit), they shall be put to death. (Exodus 22:18; Leviticus 20:27; Deuteronomy 18:10) —*The Laws and Liberties of Massachusetts,* 1641-1691, John D. Cushing, ed. (1976), 3, p. 701; 2, p. 11.

Familiar— A demon in animal form which Satan gave witches to assist them in doing harm. It might be a cat, rabbit, mouse, toad, fox, dog, bird or snake. Anyone seen in the company of such an animal, particularly a black one, might be suspected of witchcraft. The Familiar had magical powers and also served as messengers on errands for the Devil and his witches, who also had the power to transform themselves into animals to do their evil deeds. It was believed that Familiars had to receive nourishment by sucking on the body of a witch, so the accused were stripped and searched for moles, pimples, or other "witchmarks."

"Goody" — Short for the title of Goodwife, common in Colonial America. Only persons of high social rank were addessed as Mister or Mistress (or Mrs.) Most folks were called Goodman or Goodwife.

hierarchical/hierarchy — The system of ranking of officials and citizens by status and gender. Puritan New England was a hierarchy in which everyone was born into a predetermined and expected role in society.

indictment — A legal and formal accusation charging someone with a specific crime. This was presented to the court after determining whether or not there was valid evidence for trial.

malefactor — An evildoer or criminal.

malefic witch — One who caused harm through black magic or sorcery and had the ability to cause pain, sickness, despair, and death, or could destroy property and create disaster through supernatural means.

petition — A formal written request by one or more persons addressed to those in authority; a solemn document or plea meant to bring a change in some situation. A legally recognized means of protest working within the political system to bring about change.

poppet or puppet — a doll or small figure resembling a human being. The homes of suspected witches were often searched for poppets, which they supposedly fashioned after certain people they meant to harm, then twisted or stuck pins into to cause them suffering.

Puritanism — Originally a Protestant reform movement within the Church of England, the Puritans were never Separatists, like the Pilgrims who settled at Plymouth. Known then as Non-conformists, they wished for simpler worship, based upon the Bible and the teachings of John Calvin. They viewed life as a path to Salvation, filled with Satan's snares to tempt mankind who had been born into Original Sin. Persecuted in England, they came to the New World after 1629 to create "Cities of God" in the American wilderness. Theirs was a "Holy Experiment," covenanted with God, and Massachusetts Bay was fashioned upon the Old Testament. Unlike the Pilgrims, who had broken with the Anglican Church, Puritans had their own Charter and the financial backing to govern their new utopian theocracy.

specter/ spectral evidence — This was key to the Salem Trial convictions, based upon the belief that the Devil could not take human shape to afflict others, without that person's permission. Testimony that someone's specter had caused torment became crucial and admissible evidence during the Trials of 1692. There was no possible defense for the accused if someone testified to seeing his or her shape, spirit, specter, or familiar, causing harm to another person.

touch test — A ritual used to help accusers and courts discover witches, in which blind-folded suspects were brought before Afflicted person in their fits. If the touch of a suspect stopped the hysterics of the tormented ones, then that person touched might be a witch and thus, was immediately accused. This was based upon the belief that only the touch of a witch who had caused the affliction had the power to cure one who was afflicted.

warning-out — A legal Colonial system to deal with poor, transient, indigent, or undesirable persons in any New England town, so that they would not become a financial burden upon the community. From 1659 General Court entitled persons to relief after three months residence. A General Court order of 1682 allowed each town to notify such persons to leave their towns so they would not have to be responsible for the maintenance and support of such persons.

warrant — A legal writ or order providing authorities to make an arrest or property seizure for some specific crime.

wicca — A pantheistic, nature-based belief with Celtic roots, which has nothing to do with historical, Puritan concepts of witchcraft, as an evil force employed by Satan to destroy Christianity. Wicca has no devil or evil deities, but rather, celebrates gods and goddesses, devoted to the natural world and the innate goodness of humankind. 17th century New England Puritans believed in Original Sin, which meant that due to Adam's fall and Eve's temptation in the Garden of Eden, all of humanity was born to sin. Thus, Christians had to wage a constant battle to defend souls from Satan, who constantly tempted everyone off their Paths to Eternal Salvation.

About the Editor

Juliet Haines Mofford hated history in school because "it all seemed to be about men and their wars followed by treaties and more wars!" It was while studying great works of art that she discovered her profession was to be an interpreter of the past. She received her AB from Tufts University and pursued graduate studies at Boston University.

She grew up in the midwest and has lived in eleven states and six foreign countries. She has taught English and American culture in Japan, Spain and Puerto Rico, and has been a reference librarian and a museum educator. She is currently Cultural Affairs Director at the Lowell Historic Preservation Commission. Married to an English professor, she and her family spent summers camping all over the United States and Canada while their three children were growing up.

A freelance writer for twenty-five years, Juliet has published three books on New England history, two of which received national awards from the American Assocation for State and Local History. She has been a "stringer," working on assignment for *Scholastic, Inc., American History Magaine* and the *Boston Globe.* Now, as a member of The New England Speakers Bureau, she frequently lectures about the Salem Trials and other historical topics. She led a symposium on "Witchcraft at Andover" at Salem College's Tercentenary Conference in 1992. Her passion for researching old diaries, letters, probate records, and other original historical resources has led her to script writing several one-woman, "Living History" dramatic performances. Juliet is also the editor of *Talkin' Union: The American Labor Movement* in the Perspectives on History Series. She is presently working on a novel about accused "witch" Abigail Dane Faulkner.

The Perspectives on History Series